BYRON "SOULJA" BREEZE

If You Only Knew the Half

Rising Above Limits, Defying the Odds, and Embracing the Unstoppable Spirit

Contents

District of Columbia Hospital, October 23, 1973

As the rain pattered against the windows of D.C. General Hospital, cold drafts snuck in through the cracks in the aging building, brushing against the anxious faces of my family members waiting outside. I was born in this hospital as Byron Breeze Jr., but now, I go by Soulja.

Established in 1806, the District of Columbia General Hospital stood as a beacon of hope amidst the sprawling urban expanse of Washington, D.C. From the early mornings when sunlight would kiss the whitewashed brick facade of the hospital, to the dusky evenings when it cast long shadows on the bustling streets nearby, the hospital was more than a mere structure; it was a lifeline for countless residents.

The hospital held its ground on a sprawling campus that pulsed with activity. The thrum of urgency reverberated through its corridors, where the scuffed linoleum bore silent testament to the countless lives that crossed its path. Its fluorescent lights hummed overhead, casting stark shadows on the faces of nurses and doctors who navigated the labyrinthine halls, their white coats fluttering behind them.

The air inside was thick with a unique cocktail of odors: antiseptic, cafeteria food, sterilized linens, and the indefinable scent of human lives intersecting. In this diverse tapestry of sounds, smells, and sights, the DC General was more than a hospital; it was a universe unto itself, interweaving the threads of myriad narratives.

However, despite its profound importance to the community, in 2001, it became the epicenter of controversy when Mayor Anthony A. Williams decided to close its doors. The decision, a brutal blow to the public healthcare landscape of the District, was a result of a desperate attempt to cut costs while the city was on the precipice of financial ruin.

The closing sent shockwaves through the community. No longer would the echoing halls reverberate with the footsteps of dedicated medical professionals. The lights dimmed, the bustle faded, and the once vibrant lifeline of the District fell eerily silent. What once was the District's only public hospital had become a symbol of the city's struggle, its closure marking the end of an era.

My mother had received prenatal care at this hospital, including a necessary shot during her pregnancy. Little did we know, the shot would have repercussions, leaving me with a unique challenge to face. I was born without hands or legs, a tiny soldier ready to fight life's battles.

In the delivery room, my mother's sweat and tears mixed with the stench of antiseptic, painting a vivid picture of struggle and determination. The pain of childbirth was like a wildfire, spreading through her body, but she fought through it, her love for me unwavering.

The doctor looked into her eyes and suggested, "Mrs. Breeze, given your baby's condition, we could arrange for him to be placed in a specialized home."

My mother held me close, feeling the thump of her heartbeat

against my fragile body. Her voice was firm, the sound of a lioness protecting her cub. "No, he's coming home with me. We'll face this together."

Her strength, her determination, and the tenacity in her voice all became a part of me. With every breath, I felt her strength course through my veins, fortifying my resolve.

This is the story of my life: the challenges, triumphs, and the unwavering love of a mother who refused to let anything hold her child back. I may have entered this world as half a soldier, but with each passing day, I grew stronger, ready to soldier up and face whatever life had in store.

My name is Byron "Soulja" Breeze. And this is my story.

My Beautiful Strong Mother

The Unwavering Spirit

From the moment I was born, my life was never ordinary. Born without hands and legs, only my thumbs, I came into this world with a unique set of challenges that would shape the person I would become. As I grew, I discovered that life would not be easy, but I was determined to rise above my circumstances and prove to myself and the world that I could do anything I set my mind to. This memoir is not just my story; it is a testament to the resilience of the human spirit and a collection of lessons I've learned throughout my life. One of the most significant lessons I've learned is to never give up.

Growing up with a disability, I quickly realized that the world wasn't designed with me in mind. Simple tasks like getting dressed, eating, and moving around the house required tremendous effort and innovation on my part. But with each obstacle I faced, I became more determined to find ways to adapt and thrive. I learned to use my thumbs in extraordinary ways, turning them into versatile tools that allowed me to perform tasks most people take for granted. Every time I encountered a challenge, I refused to let it defeat me. I discovered the power of persistence and the importance of never giving up.

Throughout my childhood, I faced countless challenges and setbacks. There were moments of frustration and despair when I questioned if I would ever be able to live a "normal" life. But time and time again, I proved to myself that I was more than my disability. I refused to let it define me or limit my potential. Instead, I chose to focus on my abilities and what I could achieve. This mindset transformed my life and allowed me to overcome seemingly insurmountable obstacles.

My unwavering determination to never give up has been the driving force behind many of my accomplishments. I've competed in adaptive sports, pursued my education, and built a successful career. Along the way, I've encountered people who doubted my abilities or underestimated my resolve, but their skepticism only fueled my motivation to succeed. Through it all, I've learned that with persistence, creativity, and a positive mindset, there's nothing I can't achieve.

The lesson of never giving up is one that I believe everyone can benefit from, regardless of their circumstances. Life will always present challenges, but it is our response to these challenges that determines our success and happiness. By refusing to give up in the face of adversity, we can overcome our limitations and achieve our dreams. I hope that my story inspires you to embrace your own challenges and to never give up on yourself. Remember, if you only knew the half, you'd see that anything is possible with determination and perseverance.

No Excuses, Just Life

As I navigated my way through the twists and turns of life, I realized that my disability could either become my greatest excuse or my strongest motivation. I could easily succumb to self-pity and allow my circumstances to dictate my life, or I could choose to rise above them and forge my own path. I made a conscious decision early on to live a life without excuses, embracing every challenge that came my way as an opportunity to grow and evolve.

One of the most important lessons I've learned from living with a disability is that there are no excuses. Life doesn't pause for us to catch up; it keeps moving forward, and we must find ways to adapt and keep up. I discovered that the best way to face my challenges was to confront them head-on, with a positive attitude and a belief in my own abilities.

There were times when my disability made it tempting to find reasons not to pursue my dreams. It would have been easy to tell myself that I couldn't achieve certain goals because of my physical limitations. But I refused to let my circumstances dictate my life. Instead, I sought out opportunities to prove that I could succeed in spite of my disability. I pushed myself to try new activities, learn new skills, and reach for goals that seemed impossible.

One of the most significant moments in my journey was when I decided to participate in adaptive sports. I knew that I would face physical challenges, but I also recognized that this was an opportunity to prove to myself and others that there were no excuses for not living life to the fullest. Through adaptive sports, I discovered a new level of confidence and determination that carried over into other aspects of my life.

My decision to live without excuses allowed me to develop a strong work ethic and a relentless drive to succeed. I pursued my education with vigor, earning a degree despite the challenges I faced as a student with a disability. I have built a successful career, using my unique perspective to help others overcome their own obstacles.

The lesson of living without excuses is one that can benefit anyone, regardless of their circumstances. By refusing to let challenges and setbacks define our lives, we can take control of our destinies and create the lives we want. It's essential to understand that life will never be perfect, and there will always be obstacles to overcome. But by refusing to make excuses and choosing to face challenges head-on, we can achieve our dreams and live a life filled with purpose and fulfillment.

As you continue to read my story, I hope that you will find inspiration in my determination to live without excuses. Remember that the only limitations we truly have are the ones we place on ourselves. Embrace your challenges, and let them propel you forward, knowing that you are capable of overcoming anything life throws your way.

Life Happening For Me, Not To Me

As I embarked on my journey of personal transformation, I came to understand that my perspective on life would shape my experiences and my ability to overcome adversity. I learned that by shifting my mindset from one of victimhood to one of empowerment, I could view life as happening for me, rather than to me. This subtle but profound change in perspective allowed me to embrace my disability as a unique opportunity for growth and self-discovery, rather than a burden that held me back.

For much of my early life, it was easy to feel as though my disability was something that happened to me, an unfair obstacle that I was forced to endure. But as I grew older and began to face the challenges that life presented, I realized that I had a choice in how I viewed my situation. I could either continue to see my disability as something that happened to me or choose to see it as something that happened for me, a catalyst for personal growth and resilience.

By choosing to view life as happening for me, I began to see the opportunities hidden within the challenges I faced. My disability, which had once seemed like a barrier to living a fulfilling life, became a powerful teacher, showing me the value of persistence, adaptability, and self-belief. I learned to celebrate my unique abilities and to view my differences as strengths rather than limitations.

This shift in perspective allowed me to approach life with a sense of curiosity and excitement, eager to see what lessons each new experience had to teach me. I began to view every challenge as an opportunity to learn and grow, rather than as a setback or an obstacle to be overcome. This mindset transformed the way I interacted with the world, opening doors that I never knew existed and empowering me to take control of my destiny.

The lesson of looking at life as happening for me, rather than to me, is one that can benefit everyone, regardless of their circumstances. By shifting our perspective from one of victimhood to one of empowerment, we can take control of our lives and find the strength to overcome any challenge that comes our way.

I hope that you will find inspiration in my journey of personal transformation and the lessons I've learned along the way. Remember that life is happening for you, not to you, and that every challenge you face is an opportunity to grow and become the person you were meant to be. Embrace your journey, and know that you have the power to overcome adversity and create a life filled with purpose and meaning.

Keep Moving and Persevering

Throughout my life, I have encountered numerous challenges, but the key to my success has always been my unwavering commitment to keep moving and persevering. The power of perseverance, coupled with a relentless drive to adapt and improve, has propelled me forward on my journey of personal transformation and overcoming adversity. In this chapter, I share how this lesson has shaped my life and the experiences that have taught me the value of perseverance.

There have been moments in my life when it would have been easier to simply give up, to accept my limitations, and to stop pushing forward. But I knew that if I wanted to live a life filled with purpose and accomplishment, I needed to keep moving, regardless of the obstacles in my path. I understood that the only way to truly fail was to stop trying, and so I made the conscious decision to never give up on myself or my dreams.

One of the most challenging periods of my life was when I was learning to navigate the world using a wheelchair. At first, it was frustrating and disheartening, as I struggled to adapt to my new mode of transportation. But I refused to let my disability define me or dictate my future. I pushed myself to practice and improve, and over time, I gained a level of independence and freedom that I had never thought possible.

The power of perseverance has also been instrumental in my academic and professional pursuits. I faced many challenges as a student with a disability, but I refused to let these challenges deter me from achieving my goals. Through hard work, determination, and a willingness to adapt, I earned my degree and built a successful career.

In addition to my personal achievements, I have witnessed the power of perseverance in the lives of those around me. I have been inspired by the stories of others who have overcome adversity, and their determination to keep moving forward in the face of seemingly insurmountable challenges. These stories serve as a powerful reminder that we all have the ability to overcome the obstacles that life presents us, as long as we are willing to keep moving and persevering.

The lesson of keeping moving and persevering is one that can benefit everyone, regardless of their circumstances. Life is filled with challenges and setbacks, but it is how we respond to these challenges that defines our success and happiness. By refusing to give up in the face of adversity and choosing to keep moving forward, we can achieve our dreams and live a life filled with meaning and purpose.

I hope that you find inspiration in my unwavering commitment to keep moving and persevering. Remember that the only way to truly fail is to stop trying, and that you have the power to overcome any challenge that life presents you. Embrace your journey, and let your perseverance be the driving force behind your success.

Anything is Possible

Throughout my journey, I've learned that the human spirit is incredibly resilient and that anything is possible if you put your mind to it. With a combination of determination, creativity, and a willingness to adapt, I've been able to overcome seemingly insurmountable challenges and achieve things that others might have deemed impossible. In this chapter, I share my experiences and the moments that have shown me the power of believing in oneself and the endless possibilities that life has to offer.

Growing up with a disability, it was easy to focus on the things I couldn't do, rather than the things I could. But as I began to challenge myself and push the boundaries of what I thought was possible, I discovered a newfound sense of empowerment and potential. I learned that the only limitations I truly faced were the ones I placed on myself and that by believing in my own abilities, I could achieve anything I set my mind to.

One of the most defining moments in my life was when I decided to participate in adaptive sports. At first, the idea seemed daunting and even a little far-fetched, considering my physical limitations. But I refused to let my disability hold me back. I approached the challenge with an open mind and a determination to succeed, and in the process, I discovered that anything was possible if I put my mind to it.

My experiences in adaptive sports not only showed me the power of self-belief but also instilled in me a sense of confidence and self-worth that carried over into other aspects of my life. I began to approach every new challenge and opportunity with a mindset of possibility, knowing that I was capable of overcoming any obstacle and achieving any goal.

This belief in the power of possibility has been a driving force behind many of my personal and professional accomplishments. From earning my degree to building a successful career, I have consistently proven to myself and others that anything is possible if you put your mind to it. I have used my unique perspective and experiences to inspire and help others, showing them that they too can overcome adversity and achieve their dreams.

The lesson of believing in the power of possibility is one that can benefit everyone, regardless of their circumstances. By embracing a mindset of possibility and refusing to place limitations on ourselves, we can achieve our dreams and live a life filled with purpose, meaning, and happiness.

I hope that you find inspiration in my unwavering belief in the power of possibility. Remember that anything is possible if you put your mind to it, and that you have the power to overcome any challenge that life presents you. Embrace your journey and let the endless possibilities of life inspire you to reach for the stars.

Have Faith in God

Throughout my life, I have experienced the power of faith in God, which has been an essential part of my journey of personal transformation and overcoming adversity. In this chapter, I share how my faith has provided me with strength, guidance, and a sense of purpose, even in the most challenging moments of my life.

Growing up with a disability, I often found myself questioning why I had been dealt such a difficult hand in life. It was during these moments of doubt and uncertainty that I turned to my faith for comfort and understanding. As I deepened my connection with God, I began to recognize that my disability was not a punishment, but rather an opportunity to grow, learn, and inspire others.

My faith in God has been a source of unwavering support and strength throughout my life. In times of struggle, I have found solace in prayer and reflection, knowing that God was with me every step of the way. My faith has provided me with the courage to face my challenges head-on and to never give up, even when the odds seemed insurmountable.

As I continued to navigate my journey, I began to see the hand of God at work in my life, guiding me towards opportunities and experiences that have shaped who I am today. From participating in adaptive sports to pursuing my education and career, I have witnessed the power of faith in God, which has opened doors and led me down paths I never could have imagined.

Beyond the personal strength and guidance that my faith has provided, it has also allowed me to connect with others on a deeper level. Through my faith, I have found a community of like-minded individuals who have supported and encouraged me on my journey. I have also had the opportunity to share my story and my faith with others, inspiring them to overcome their own challenges and to trust in God's plan for their lives.

The lesson of having faith in God is one that can benefit everyone, regardless of their circumstances. By trusting in a higher power and seeking guidance and strength from our faith, we can find the courage and resilience needed to face life's challenges and to embrace our unique journeys.

I hope that you find inspiration in my faith and the role it has played in my journey of personal transformation and overcoming adversity. Remember that by having faith in God, you can find the strength and guidance needed to overcome any challenge that life presents you. Embrace your journey and let your faith in God be your guiding light as you navigate the twists and turns of life.

The Green Light at the End of the Tunnel

I n my journey of personal transformation and overcoming adversity, I have come to understand that no matter how big the obstacle, there is always a green light at the end of the tunnel. In this chapter, I share the experiences that have taught me the importance of maintaining hope and optimism, even in the face of seemingly insurmountable challenges.

Throughout my life, I have faced numerous obstacles, both physical and emotional, that have tested my resilience and determination. From learning to navigate the world with a disability to confronting societal attitudes and misconceptions, there have been moments when the path before me seemed dark and uncertain. But with each challenge, I have found the strength to persevere, buoyed by the belief that there is always a green light at the end of the tunnel.

This unyielding optimism and hope have been instrumental in helping me overcome adversity and achieve my goals. By focusing on the positive and maintaining a sense of hope, I have been able to push through the most difficult moments and emerge stronger and more resilient on the other side.

One of the most significant moments in my life that demon-strated the power of this belief was when I pursued my education. Facing accessibility challenges and societal prejudices, there were times when it seemed as though the odds were stacked against me. But I refused to give up, and with each small victory, I could see the green light at the end of the tunnel growing brighter.

My experiences have taught me that the green light at the end of the tunnel is not a distant, unattainable goal, but rather a beacon of hope that we carry within ourselves. By maintaining a sense of optimism and hope, we can find the strength and resilience needed to overcome any obstacle and to keep moving forward on our journey.

The lesson of believing in the green light at the end of the tunnel is one that can benefit everyone, regardless of their circumstances. Life is filled with challenges and setbacks, but it is our ability to maintain hope and optimism in the face of adversity that defines our success and happiness.

Please find inspiration in my unwavering belief in the green light at the end of the tunnel. Remember that no matter how big the obstacle, there is always a beacon of hope and possibility waiting for you, as long as you are willing to persevere and keep moving forward. Embrace your journey and let the green light guide you towards a brighter and more fulfilling future.

Like Reaching Out to a Friend

In my journey of personal transformation and overcoming adversity, I have come to appreciate the importance of human connections and the simple act of reaching out to a friend. In this chapter, I share how staying true to my word and nurturing friendships has enriched my life and supported me through the challenges I have faced.

The power of friendship is often underestimated, but it is through these connections that we find the strength and support we need to face life's challenges. Just as important as cultivating these relationships is the act of staying true to our word and following through on our promises.

One of the most valuable lessons I've learned in my life is the importance of being reliable and honoring my commitments to others. If I say I'm going to call a friend, I make sure to do so, not only because it strengthens our bond, but also because it helps build trust and demonstrates that I genuinely care.

There have been countless moments when a simple phone call or message from a friend has lifted my spirits and provided me with the encouragement I needed to persevere through difficult times. In turn, I have made it a priority to be there for my friends when they need me, offering a listening ear or a shoulder to lean on. By staying true to my word and reaching out to my friends, I have forged relationships that have become a crucial source of support and inspiration.

Through my experiences, I have come to understand that our friendships are like a lifeline, a connection that provides us with strength and comfort in the face of adversity. By making an effort to reach out to our friends and honoring our commitments to them, we not only nurture these relationships but also create a network of support that can help carry us through even the most difficult moments in our lives.

The lesson of reaching out to a friend and staying true to our word is one that can benefit everyone, regardless of their circumstances. By cultivating and nurturing our friendships, we can build a strong foundation of support that can help us overcome life's challenges and setbacks.

Reading my story, I hope that you find inspiration in the value I place on friendships and the simple act of reaching out. Remember that by honoring your commitments and staying true to your word, you can foster strong and lasting relationships that will provide you with the support and encouragement you need to navigate life's twists and turns. Embrace your journey and let the power of friendship guide you towards a richer, more fulfilling life.

My Badge of Honor: No Excuses

Throughout my journey of personal transformation and overcoming adversity, I have embraced a "no excuses" mentality that has become my badge of honor. In this chapter, I share how this mindset has empowered me to face my challenges head-on and achieve my goals, no matter the obstacles that may stand in my way.

Living with a disability has presented me with numerous challenges and limitations, but I have always refused to let these obstacles define me or hold me back. I carry the "no excuses" mindset like a badge of honor, as it constantly reminds me of my strength, resilience, and determination to live life on my own terms.

The "no excuses" mentality has served as a source of empowerment, pushing me to take responsibility for my actions and to make the most of every opportunity that comes my way. Instead of dwelling on my limitations or feeling sorry for myself, I have chosen to focus on my abilities and the countless possibilities that life has to offer.

This mindset has been instrumental in helping me achieve many of my personal and professional goals, from pursuing my education to participating in adaptive sports and building a successful career. By embracing the "no excuses" mentality, I have consistently proven to myself and others that I am capable of overcoming any challenge and achieving any dream I set my mind to.

The lesson of carrying the "no excuses" mindset as a badge of honor is one that can benefit everyone, regardless of their circumstances. By taking responsibility for our lives and refusing to let obstacles stand in our way, we can achieve our goals and live a life filled with purpose and meaning.

As you continue to read my journey, I hope that you find inspiration in my unwavering commitment to the "no excuses" mindset and the strength it has given me to face life's challenges. Remember that by carrying this badge of honor, you too can overcome adversity and achieve your dreams. Embrace your journey and let the "no excuses" mentality guide you towards a life filled with possibility and success.

No Excuses in Plain Sight

As I navigate through life with my disability, my presence in everyday situations, such as walking down the street, grocery shopping, or driving, serves as a powerful testament to the "no excuses" mentality that has guided me throughout my journey. In this chapter, I share the impact that my public presence has had on others and how it demonstrates that there are no excuses for not embracing life, regardless of the challenges one may face.

When people see me going about my daily activities, they often express surprise or admiration at my ability to overcome my physical limitations. My presence serves as a visual reminder that with determination, creativity, and perseverance, it is possible to adapt and thrive, even when faced with significant challenges.

My experiences in public spaces have led to numerous conversations with strangers, who often express their amazement at my independence and resilience. These interactions have allowed me to share my story and spread the message of the "no excuses" mentality that has been so integral to my personal transformation and overcoming adversity.

By living my life openly and without excuses, I hope to inspire others to face their own challenges with courage and determination. My experiences demonstrate that it is not our circumstances that define us, but rather our mindset and our willingness to adapt and persevere.

The lesson of living life without excuses and embracing our challenges is one that can benefit everyone, regardless of their circumstances. When we refuse to let our limitations hold us back and choose to face our obstacles head-on, we can live a life filled with purpose, meaning, and personal growth.

I hope and pray that you find inspiration in the way I live my life in plain sight, demonstrating the power of the "no excuses" mentality to all who encounter me. Remember that by embracing your challenges and living life without excuses, you too can overcome adversity and achieve your dreams. Embrace your journey and let the "no excuses" mindset guide you towards a life filled with possibility and success.

Making Dreams a Reality

Throughout my journey of personal transformation and overcoming adversity, I have come to believe in the power of determination and the idea that anything you want, you can make it happen. In this chapter, I share how this belief has fueled my dreams and aspirations, enabling me to defy expectations and achieve my goals.

From a young age, I have been driven by the belief that anything is possible if I set my mind to it. This conviction has been the guiding force behind my pursuit of my dreams, despite the challenges and obstacles presented by my disability. I have learned that with determination, creativity, and hard work, I can overcome any limitation and make my dreams a reality.

My experiences have shown me that the first step in making dreams come true is to believe in oneself and one's abilities. This belief fuels the determination and resilience needed to face challenges and persevere through setbacks. By embracing this mindset, I have been able to achieve many of my goals, such as pursuing my education, participating in adaptive sports, and building a successful career.

Another crucial element in making dreams a reality is to surround oneself with a supportive network of friends, family, and mentors. These individuals have played a significant role in my journey, providing encouragement, guidance, and assistance when needed. With their support, I have been able to push through barriers and achieve what may have once seemed impossible.

The lesson of believing that anything you want can be made to happen is one that can benefit everyone, regardless of their circumstances. By embracing this mindset and pursuing our dreams with determination and persistence, we can overcome obstacles and create a life filled with purpose, meaning, and personal growth.

As you continue to read my story, I hope that you find inspiration in my unwavering belief that anything is possible if you set your mind to it. Remember that by embracing this belief and pursuing your dreams with determination, you too can overcome adversity and achieve your goals. Embrace your journey and let the power of possibility guide you towards a life filled with success and happiness.

The Purpose

I n this section of my memoir, I delve into the underlying purpose behind sharing my story with the world. Like anyone's purpose in life, my goal is to make a difference – to inspire, empower, and motivate others to overcome their own challenges and embrace their unique journeys.

My memoir serves as a testament to the power of resilience and determination in the face of adversity. By sharing my experiences, struggles, and triumphs, I hope to show that it is possible to rise above limitations and live a life filled with purpose and meaning.

My story is a reminder that each of us has the potential to make a difference in our own lives and in the lives of others. Through my journey, I have learned invaluable lessons about perseverance, self-acceptance, and the importance of cultivating a positive mindset. By sharing these insights, I aim to inspire others to face their challenges with courage and to seek out their own paths to personal growth and fulfillment.

Moreover, my memoir serves as a platform for advocating for greater understanding, acceptance, and support for individuals with disabilities. By sharing my experiences and perspectives, I hope to challenge misconceptions and encourage a more inclusive and compassionate society.

The purpose of my memoir extends beyond my personal story, as it seeks to foster a sense of connection and shared humanity. My experiences demonstrate that while we all face unique challenges and circumstances, we share a common desire to make a difference in our lives and in the world around us.

As you read my memoir, I invite you to reflect on your own purpose in life and consider how you can make a difference. Embrace your journey and let the lessons and experiences shared within these pages inspire and guide you towards a life filled with purpose, meaning, and personal growth. Together, we can make a difference – one story at a time.

A Beacon of Hope and Encouragement

I want to discuss another essential purpose of my memoir: to offer hope and encouragement to others by demonstrating that anything in life is possible, and dreams can indeed come true, bringing happiness and fulfillment.

My story serves as a beacon of hope for those facing adversity, showing that even in the face of significant challenges, it is possible to achieve one's dreams and find happiness. Through my experiences, I have learned that with determination, resilience, and a positive mindset, we can overcome seemingly insurmountable obstacles and create a life that is rich in purpose and joy.

By sharing my journey, I aim to encourage others to believe in their own abilities and to pursue their dreams with unwavering conviction. Each of us has the power to shape our own destinies, and it is through our determination and perseverance that we can make our dreams a reality.

My story is not just about overcoming physical limitations; it is about the triumph of the human spirit and the potential that lies within each of us to create a life that is meaningful and fulfilling. By sharing my experiences, I hope to inspire others to embrace their own journeys and to pursue their dreams with confidence and enthusiasm.

The message of hope and encouragement that I offer in this chapter is universal, resonating with anyone who has faced challenges or adversity. We all have the potential to achieve our dreams and find happiness, and it is through our shared experiences and stories that we can inspire one another to reach for the stars.

I hope that you find inspiration in the message of hope and encouragement that I share. Embrace the belief that anything is possible, and let this conviction guide you towards a life filled with happiness, purpose, and personal growth.

A Living Inspiration

nother motivation that drives me forward in life: the desire to inspire and motivate others through my actions and determination. As I go about my daily activities, I hope that my presence in public spaces and my resilience will inspire those who encounter me to face their own challenges with courage and determination.

My disability has not stopped me from living a full and active life. Whether I am grocery shopping, driving, or participating in sports, I strive to demonstrate that limitations can be overcome with persistence, creativity, and a positive mindset. I believe that my visibility and determination can serve as a powerful source of inspiration for others, motivating them to overcome their own obstacles and pursue their dreams.

As I move through life, I am keenly aware that my actions have the potential to impact others. I carry this responsibility with pride, using it as motivation to push through barriers and continue to grow and achieve. By sharing my story and embracing my journey, I hope to inspire others to do the same, fostering a sense of community and shared resilience.

My motivation to keep moving on and inspire others is a testament to the power of human connection and the potential for personal transformation that lies within each of us. Through our shared experiences and stories, we can lift each other up, offering encouragement, support, and motivation in the face of life's challenges.

As you continue to read my memoir, I hope that you find inspiration in my determination to keep moving forward and to inspire those around me. Embrace your own journey, and let the power of your actions and determination serve as a source of motivation for others. Together, we can create a world filled with inspiration, resilience, and personal growth.

Personal Growth

In this section of my memoir, I explore the lessons I have learned about personal growth, and how reaching out to others in need of motivation and hope has played a significant role in my own journey of self-discovery and development.

One of the most profound aspects of my personal growth has been the realization of the power of connection and the impact we can have on others by offering support, encouragement, and hope. As I have navigated my own challenges, I have discovered that reaching out to others in need of motivation can be a trans formative experience, both for those we help and for ourselves.

By offering a listening ear, a helping hand, or a kind word, we can provide a lifeline for those who may be struggling to find hope and direction in their own lives. This act of compassion not only uplifts others but also enriches our own lives, fostering a sense of purpose and meaning that is essential for personal growth.

As I have reached out to others, I have learned invaluable lessons about empathy, resilience, and the importance of cultivating a positive mindset. These experiences have shaped my understanding of personal growth, teaching me that our own development is intrinsically linked to the connections we forge with others and the impact we have on their lives.

In this section, I share the stories and experiences that have shaped my personal growth and how reaching out to others in need of motivation and hope has been a crucial part of my journey. Through these stories, I hope to inspire readers to recognize the power of connection and the role it plays in our own personal development.

I encourage you to reflect on your own personal growth and consider how reaching out to others can play a role in your own journey. Embrace the power of connection and let the lessons and experiences shared within these pages guide you towards a life filled with purpose, meaning, and personal growth.

A Childhood of Dreams and Determination

I n this chapter, I delve into my childhood memories and explore how I created my own reality, dealt with my situation as a loner, and found inspiration in the stars and the endless possibilities of the universe.

Growing up in Landover, Maryland, I often found solace in my own little world. Although I had friends, I was mostly to myself, riding my skateboard around the neighborhood and embracing my unique situation. Then, a significant milestone occurred when I got fitted for prosthetic legs.

I vividly recall the moment at Friendly High School when my friends and other students saw me standing with legs for the first time. The excitement in their voices was palpable:

"Wow, look at you! Standing all tall now!" "It's amazing to see you like this. We're so happy for you!"

Despite the positive attention, I discovered that I moved around faster without the legs, so I continued to navigate the world in my own way. My childhood was marked by a strong sense of determination and independence.

During my time at Catherine T Reed Elementary School, I found comfort in a small group of friends and excelled in my studies. One particular aspect of the school that captivated me was its planetarium. Gazing up at the stars, I was endlessly fascinated by the vastness of the universe and the limitless potential it represented.

The stars and the Milky Way became a powerful source of motivation for me, symbolizing the boundless possibilities for dreams and hope. I would sit back, immersed in the cosmic spectacle, and internalize the idea that the universe is endless – much like the potential to achieve our dreams.

I pray my childhood experiences inspire you to recognize the endless potential within yourself and the importance of creating your own reality, even in the face of adversity. Let the stars and the universe serve as a reminder that there are no limits to what we can achieve if we dare to dream and persevere.

Seeds of Dreams: A Visit from Len Bias

I remember when the great Len Bias used to come over my house to see my older sister, Lisa. The six-foot-eight Maryland Terrapin would hunch under our doorway, his infectious smile lighting up the room. Even as a kid, I knew there was something larger than life about Lenny. Not just his physical presence but his spirit, the energy around him was magnetic. It was a gentle kind of spring day, the sun scattering its warmth generously, the trees humming with the arrival of new leaves, the air lightly perfumed with the scent of cherry blossoms.

"Hey, little Soulja," Len would always greet me, ruffling my hair with his massive hand. His voice was like a tune played on a well-loved piano, warm and inviting.

One day, as we sat on our porch, the mild breeze making the wind chime tinkle melodically, I gathered my courage and asked him, "Len, would you come and speak to my elementary school class?"

He looked down at me, surprise lighting his features, "Oh, yeah? Your class, huh? And what should I talk about?"

"Motivation," I answered, my heart hammering in my chest. "About being who you want to be when you grow up."

He let out a hearty laugh, eyes crinkling at the corners. "All right, little Soulja," he said, giving my shoulder a squeeze. "I can do that."

When the day arrived, Len towered over my classmates in our tiny classroom, his deep voice filling every corner. The weather outside was perfect, just like the day I asked him. A sunny optimism hung in the room like a promise, and I could almost taste the anticipation in the air.

"Kids," he began, his voice filling the room, "you can become anyone you want. The world is like a giant field, and your dreams are the seeds. All you need is the motivation to tend to them, water them, and let them grow."

As he spoke, the classroom fell into a hushed silence. The usual shuffling of feet, the whispers, the occasional giggling, all ceased. Even the outside world seemed to pause, the birds in the trees quieting their songs to listen in.

"Do you know what the best part about dreams is?" He continued, looking around at the sea of young, eager faces. "They can come true. No dream is too big, no aspiration too high."

The metaphor of dreams and seeds bloomed in the room,

wrapping around each child like a cocoon of possibilities. The world suddenly expanded, stretching out into horizons of 'could be' and 'would be.' In that moment, we were no longer just kids in a small classroom in D.C.; we were astronauts, presidents, athletes, writers, artists, dreamers, every aspiration hanging within reach.

It's one thing to hear about motivation, but it's another to see it in flesh and blood. Len Bias, a living example of ambition and hard work, stood amidst us, sprinkling seeds of dreams in the fertile soil of young minds. And as I watched my classmates' faces, eyes wide, mouths slightly open, I knew those seeds were already starting to sprout.

LEN BIAS
November 18, 1963-June 19, 1986
Continue Resting in Peace & Paradise My Friend

Embracing the Challenge: My Special Olympics Journey

I want to recount my experiences participating in the Special Olympics and the impact it had on my life. Through getting involved in various events, meeting people with similar challenges, and embracing the spirit of competition, I discovered a supportive community and a renewed sense of purpose.

Joining the Special Olympics was an opportunity to connect with others who faced similar challenges, forging friendships and gaining a deeper understanding of the unique experiences we all shared. The atmosphere of camaraderie, support, and encouragement was truly inspiring.

I eagerly participated in events such as the wheelchair race and the skateboard race, pushing my physical limits and experiencing the thrill of competition. The Special Olympics featured a diverse range of events, attracting participants from schools with special needs classes and providing us all with a platform to showcase our talents and determination.

The events were structured to recognize the efforts and achievements of participants, with awards given for 1st, 2nd, and 3rd place. This aspect of the Special Olympics was particularly meaningful for me, as it offered something to strive for and a sense of accomplishment when goals were met.

Looking back on my involvement in the Special Olympics, I can see how it played a vital role in my personal growth and development. The experience not only provided me with an outlet for my competitive spirit but also taught me valuable lessons about perseverance, sportsmanship, and the power of community.

I hope my experiences with the Special Olympics inspire you to embrace challenges and seek out opportunities for personal growth, regardless of the obstacles you may face. Through competition and camaraderie, we can find strength, support, and a renewed sense of purpose in our lives.

Pushing For the Gold

Discovering Passions: My Middle School Adventures

Reflecting on my experiences in middle school, where I explored various interests and discovered a passion for hands-on activities. Through classes such as metal shop, cooking, and wood shop, I began to envision my future and develop skills that would serve me throughout my life.

Middle school offered a diverse range of classes designed to help students discover their interests and prepare for their future careers. I eagerly embraced the opportunity to participate in metal shop, where I learned the basics of working with metal and developed an appreciation for craftsmanship.

Cooking classes allowed me to explore my culinary creativity and develop skills that would prove invaluable in my day-to-day life. These classes also taught me the importance of self-reliance and resourcefulness – qualities that would become integral to my journey of personal growth.

My favorite class, however, was wood shop. I was captivated by the process of transforming raw materials into functional and beautiful objects, and I found great satisfaction in working with my hands to create something from nothing. One memorable project involved building race cars – an experience that brought together my love for craftsmanship and my competitive spirit.

As I progressed through middle school, these classes provided me with a solid foundation of practical skills and instilled in me a sense of curiosity and determination. They also helped me envision a future in which I could use my creativity and resourcefulness to overcome challenges and pursue my passions.

Reading this chapter, I hope my middle school experiences inspire you to explore your own interests and pursue your passions, no matter the challenges you may face. Through hands-on learning and personal growth, we can unlock our potential and create a fulfilling and meaningful life.

Lessons Beyond the Classroom: My Friendly High School Experience

Looking back on my time at Friendly High School, where I formed lasting friendships and learned valuable lessons outside the traditional classroom setting. Despite feeling rushed through the educational process, I found that my connections with my peers ultimately shaped my growth and understanding.

During my years at Friendly High School, I met many friends who would remain in my life for years to come. The bonds we forged extended beyond the school walls and provided a strong support network that helped me navigate the challenges of adolescence and beyond.

As for my academic experience, I felt that the learning process was somewhat rushed. Rather than focusing on mastering subjects and acquiring a deep understanding, it often felt like I was being pushed through the system. This left me with a sense that my education was incomplete, and I yearned for more knowledge and understanding.

However, I discovered that some of the most valuable lessons came from my interactions with my peers. By learning from their experiences, insights, and perspectives, I gained a broader understanding of the world and developed a strong sense of empathy and resilience. These lessons from my fellow students proved to be as important, if not more so, than the formal education I received.

My high school journey took a slight detour when I graduated in 1992 instead of 1991 as originally planned. Despite this setback, I embraced the opportunity to continue learning and growing, both in and out of the classroom.

I pray my experiences at Friendly High School encourage you to recognize the value of learning from your peers and the importance of building strong connections. The lessons we learn outside the classroom can be just as important as those we learn within, shaping our lives in profound and lasting ways.

The Universal Language: How Math Shaped My Life

Exploring the lasting impact of my education and how, despite feeling unprepared for the realities of today's world, one subject in particular – mathematics – has had a profound influence on my life.

Reflecting on my schooling, I recognize that many of the lessons I learned did not adequately prepare me for the complexities and challenges of today's world. The rapid pace of change and the emergence of new technologies and global issues have left many of us feeling unprepared and uncertain about the future.

However, amidst this sea of change, I discovered that one subject has remained a constant source of guidance and clarity: math. Mathematics is a universal language that transcends cultural and geographical boundaries, providing a foundation for critical thinking and problem-solving in almost every aspect of our lives.

From managing personal finances to understanding the world around us, math plays a crucial role in our daily existence. It has taught me the importance of precision, logical reasoning, and the ability to analyze situations from multiple angles. These skills have enabled me to navigate the challenges of life with greater confidence and resilience.

Mathematics has also offered me a sense of order and stability in an ever-changing world, reinforcing the belief that there are underlying patterns and connections that govern the universe. This appreciation for the beauty and elegance of math has deepened my understanding of the world and fueled my desire to learn and grow.

Reading this chapter, I hope that my experiences with mathematics inspire you to recognize the value and relevance of this subject in your own life. By embracing the lessons and wisdom offered by math, we can better navigate the complexities of today's world and empower ourselves to live more fulfilling and purposeful lives.

Reigniting the Flame: Returning to the Special Olympics in High School

Recounting my experience rejoining the Special Olympics during high school, after a brief hiatus in junior high. The return to this familiar and cherished event rekindled my competitive spirit and provided a sense of purpose during a tumultuous time in my life.

Upon entering high school, I was delighted to discover that the

Special Olympics were once again part of my academic journey. The event held a special place in my heart, not only for the sense of camaraderie it fostered but also for the opportunity it provided to challenge myself and others in friendly competition.

Reconnecting with the Special Olympics in high school brought back the exhilaration of competition and the joy of pushing my physical limits. It served as a reminder of my resilience and determination, qualities that had shaped my life and allowed me to overcome seemingly insurmountable obstacles.

Despite the positive impact of the Special Olympics, my high school years remain somewhat of a blur in my memory. The whirlwind of emotions, friendships, and personal growth that characterized this period can be difficult to recall in precise detail. However, the enduring influence of the Special Olympics and the lessons it taught me have remained a constant source of inspiration and motivation.

I hope and pray that my experiences with the Special Olympics during high school encourage you to recognize the importance of maintaining your passions and staying connected to the activities that bring out the best in you. By embracing the challenges and opportunities that life presents, we can forge a path toward personal growth and self-discovery.

Seeking Belonging and the True Purpose of Education

In this chapter, I explore my struggle to fit in with my peers during my school years and share my thoughts on the true purpose of education – to prepare young people for adulthood and equip them with the necessary skills to navigate the world.

Like many adolescents, I grappled with the desire to blend in and be accepted by my peers. This quest for belonging often took precedence over my academic pursuits, as I navigated the complex social dynamics of school life. While forming connections and friendships is a valuable part of personal growth, I couldn't help but wonder if the focus on fitting in distracted me from more important aspects of my education.

As I reflect on my schooling, I believe that the primary goal of education should be to prepare students for the challenges and responsibilities of adulthood. This means going beyond the traditional curriculum and instilling in young people the skills and values they will need to succeed in the world, such as critical thinking, empathy, and resilience.

In my experience, the education system often fell short in this regard, prioritizing rote memorization and standardized testing over the development of well-rounded individuals. I believe that by shifting the focus of education toward personal growth and practical skills, we can better prepare young people for the realities of adult life.

Reading this chapter, I hope that my reflections on fitting in and the purpose of education resonate with you and spark a conversation about the true goals of learning. By reimagining the education system and placing a greater emphasis on personal growth and real-world skills, we can empower future generations to lead fulfilling and meaningful lives.

The Storm Within: Battle Against Betrayal

I felt like I was about to get sick, so I excused myself and went to the bathroom. It got worse when I got to the bathroom, to a point where I couldn't move. The linoleum tiles below me felt cold and indifferent, a stark contrast to the storm that was raging within my body. The fair weather outside was a cruel joke, mocking the tempest I was experiencing internally.

A sheen of sweat broke out on my forehead as I clung to the toilet. My stomach was turning, a rebellious sea refusing to calm down. The fluorescent lights overhead buzzed like an annoyed wasp, heightening my discomfort.

Suddenly, the door creaked open. "Soulja? You okay in here?" My brother's voice echoed in the eerie silence. The concern was palpable in his tone.

"No... I can't... can't move." My words came out as a faint whisper, a cry for help.

He was by my side in an instant, his face etched with worry. "Hang on, Soulja. I *got* you, I'm gonna call 911."

My body was a battlefield, a war waged by unseen assailants, attacking my kidneys with relentless fury. The pain wasn't just physical anymore; it was a betrayal, a silent mutiny by my own organs. My kidneys, once faithful soldiers, had become traitors plotting my downfall.

As I was loaded onto the ambulance, the sun was shining incongruously in the clear sky, the cool breeze lazily rustling the leaves in the trees lining Friendly High School. The world seemed indifferent to my agony, carrying on its normal routine under the fair weather.

At Washington Hospital Center, the verdict came: kidney failure. The words echoed in my mind, a jarring reminder of the body's fallibility. My body had revolted, and in the aftermath of the rebellion, I was left with a solitary soldier, one kidney standing guard where two had once been.

In the cruel light of day, my world had been irrevocably changed. The fair weather was a stark contrast to my internal storm. But this was my reality now, a new chapter in the relentless saga of my life.

An Unlikely Friendship: The Story of Daryl Spencer and Me

I would love to share the story of my gym teacher, Daryl Spencer, and the unusual way our friendship began. Daryl was a dedicated advocate for special needs students and played an instrumental role in helping us participate in the Special Olympics. Through a memorable encounter, we formed a lasting bond that would stand the test of time.

I can still remember the day Daryl and I first crossed paths. It was just another ordinary day at school, and I was on my way to class in my wheelchair. Daryl, who was always eager to lend a helping hand, noticed me struggling to make it to class on time. In his haste to help, he grabbed the handles of my wheelchair and began pushing me with great force.

As we sped down the hallway, disaster struck. My thumb became caught between the wheel and the chair, causing me immense pain. Unable to contain my frustration, I let out a string of expletives and lashed out at Daryl for his overzealous assistance. The incident landed me a one-day suspension, but it also marked the beginning of a unique and lasting friendship.

Over time, Daryl and I grew to understand and appreciate each other. Our initial encounter, while far from ideal, taught us valuable lessons about communication and empathy. Daryl learned to be more mindful of the needs and boundaries of the students he worked with, while I gained a better understanding of the intentions behind his actions.

Our shared experiences in the Special Olympics further cemented our bond, as we worked together to help our fellow special needs students achieve their goals. Through the ups and downs, triumphs and setbacks, Daryl and I remained steadfast friends and confidants.

I hope and pray that the story of my friendship with Daryl Spencer inspires you to appreciate the unlikely connections and life lessons that can arise from challenging experiences. In the face of adversity, true friendships can blossom and serve as a testament to the power of understanding, empathy, and perseverance.

Breaking Barriers: Finding Success in the Face of Adversity

I want to recount my journey to financial independence and the challenges I faced along the way due to my disability. Despite the obstacles presented by a world not always designed with my needs in mind, I persevered and found a way to make a living on my own terms.

Finding work as a person with a disability can be a daunting task, as many employers are hesitant to hire someone who may require accommodations or assistance. I quickly discovered that conventional job hunting strategies were not yielding the results I had hoped for, and I knew I had to take matters into my own hands.

Determined to carve out my own path to success, I began exploring alternative ways to generate income. Through a combination of ingenuity, hard work, and persistence, I managed to create a steady stream of revenue that not only supported me financially but also granted me a sense of accomplishment and self-sufficiency.

This journey was by no means an easy one, and it required a great deal of self-motivation and resilience. There were days when the obstacles seemed insurmountable, but I knew I could not afford to give in to despair. I had to dig deep and find the strength to keep moving forward, trusting in my abilities and refusing to let my disability define my worth.

Overcoming adversity in the pursuit of financial independence can inspire you to challenge the limits that others may place on you. Remember that you are the master of your own destiny, and with determination, creativity, and perseverance, you can achieve your goals and prove that anything is possible.

Caught in the Eye of Accusation

I thought a tornado was trying to bust up into my apartment, the way the door violently shook, and then crashed open with a deafening bang. The day had started innocently enough, the sky a radiant blue, the air crisp and clean. But suddenly, my world twisted into a tempest.

"It's the police!" a voice thundered through the chaotic gusts of fear, ripping through my apartment like a violent storm. The tranquility of the morning had turned treacherous, mirroring the tornado of accusation swirling around me.

"Mr. Breeze!" one of the officers bellowed, his voice echoing in the now chaotic space. "You are under arrest for conspiracy to commit organized crime!"

I stood, my back against the wall as they stormed in, their boots thumping on the wooden floor like a gruesome drumline, their presence an unforgiving whirlwind. Their uniforms, blue as the deceiving sky outside, seemed out of place in my humble abode. "Conspiracy?" I managed to choke out, my voice hoarse, "There must be some mistake."

A muscular officer, his face hidden behind dark sunglasses, handcuffed me. "No mistake, Mr. Breeze. We've been watching you, watching the company you keep."

He was stern, unyielding, like a hard, wooden shampoo, scrubbing away at my integrity, my dignity, my rights. The comparison may seem absurd, but in that moment, the metaphor was fitting. They were here to cleanse me of my presumed guilt, to purify their city from the likes of me, to restore order from the tornado they claimed I was part of.

"But I've done nothing wrong!" I protested, the metallic taste of panic spreading in my mouth. The apartment was filled with cold authority and the sharp smell of fear. The sound of my protests was drowned out by the radio chatter, the crackle of their walkie-talkies like a distress signal in a storm.

They rifled through my belongings, my life, looking for evidence of the storm they accused me of brewing. The invasion was as destructive and ruthless as a tornado, leaving a path of wreckage in its wake. The scene was a storm of chaos, my life being thrown into disarray before my very eyes.

Through it all, I stood firm in the eye of the storm, the calm epicenter, clinging to my innocence. A tornado might have been tearing through my apartment, but it would not rip apart my resolve. The storm would pass, I told myself. And when it did, they'd realize they'd been chasing the wrong wind.

63

The Path to Self-Reliance: Choosing a Different Road

In this chapter, I discuss the importance of self-reliance and the choices I made to avoid falling into a dangerous lifestyle. I learned that no organization or group would save me – I had to take responsibility for my own life and make better decisions for my future.

Emerging from high school and facing the harsh realities of the world, I found myself struggling to find my footing. With limited opportunities and support, I resorted to hustling and engaging in activities that I knew were wrong. Although I never got caught or faced serious consequences, I saw friends get into trouble, and I realized that continuing down this path would only lead to more problems.

Recognizing the risks associated with my choices, I made the conscious decision to change my trajectory. I understood that no external force or organization was going to save me; I needed to take control of my life and make better choices for my own well-being.

This realization marked a turning point in my journey, as I began to seek out alternative means of supporting myself and building a stable, fulfilling life. By taking responsibility for my actions and decisions, I was able to break free from the cycle of destructive behavior and focus on overcoming the obstacles that stood between me and my dreams.

Reading this chapter, I hope that my story of self-reliance and the decision to forge a different path serves as a reminder that we are ultimately responsible for our own lives. With determination, courage, and a strong sense of self-worth, we can choose to break free from negative patterns and create a brighter future for ourselves.

Swallowing Pride: A Bittersweet Path to Financial Stability

In this chapter, I delve into the complex emotions surrounding my experience of accepting financial help from strangers, a decision I had initially resisted but ultimately embraced in pursuit of financial stability. This decision, though lucrative, also forced me to confront my pride and reassess my goals for the future.

As I went about my daily routines, I noticed people offering me money, often with kind words about my resilience and determination. At first, I saw these gestures as disrespectful and rejected their generosity, unwilling to accept pity from others.

However, my cousin Greg Hamilton saw things differently. He convinced me to visit him in New York, where he assured me I could make a considerable amount of money simply by being present in public spaces. To my surprise, he was right; in just one day, I made almost two thousand dollars without saying a word to anyone.

This experience was both gratifying and uncomfortable. As a child, I hated being stared at and having my picture taken by strangers, and the thought of capitalizing on the attention my disability attracted filled me with mixed emotions. Yet, faced with the reality of my financial situation, I chose to swallow my pride and do what was necessary to support myself.

Despite the financial success I found through this unconventional means, I knew in my heart that it was not a sustainable or fulfilling path for me. As I continued to receive money from strangers, I resolved to seek out new avenues for income and personal growth, determined to create a better future for myself on my own terms.

My story of embracing the difficult choice to accept help from others I hope will inspire you to reflect on your own values and priorities. While we all must make sacrifices and compromises to survive, it is equally important to never lose sight of our true goals and aspirations.

Three Strikes: Navigating the Challenges of Identity and Disability

I want to explore my three strikes. The concept of being born with "three strikes" against me – my disability, my race, and my gender – and how these factors have shaped my experiences and perception of the world. Despite the challenges, I have found support in unexpected places and maintain a strong faith in a higher power.

Growing up, I always felt that I was born with three strikes against me. Strike one: I was born disabled. Strike two: I was black. And strike three: I was a black male. These factors combined to create a set of unique challenges that made it difficult for me to find my place in the world. No matter which path I tried to take, I found that doors were often closed to me, and opportunities were limited.

Despite these challenges, I have always been determined to push through and overcome the obstacles in my way. Along the way, I have encountered people who have offered help and support, often appearing unexpectedly and seeming to be sent by a higher power. These individuals have helped me believe in the possibility of a better future, despite the hurdles I faced.

As I reflect on my life's journey, I am reminded of the strength and resilience it takes to navigate the world with these three strikes against me. But instead of allowing them to define me or limit my potential, I have chosen to see them as part of the unique tapestry of my life, offering me the opportunity to grow, learn, and inspire others.

I pray that my story of perseverance in the face of adversity encourages you to confront your own challenges head-on and to find the strength within yourself to overcome the obstacles that may stand in your way.

The Struggle to Thrive – Disability, Finances, and Resilience

Struggling to thrive and survive out here, I want to delve into the financial challenges of living with a disability and the pressure to remain dependent on disability checks, while still striving for independence and self-sufficiency.

Growing up, the one thing I could always count on was my disability check. However, this financial support came with its own set of limitations. Whenever I tried to earn additional income or create new opportunities for myself, I would often face the threat of having my disability checks taken away. This led to a constant struggle to balance my desire for independence and self-sufficiency with the need to maintain a secure source of income.

Now that I am approaching 50, the challenges remain. Any increases in my disability and social security benefits are minimal, barely enough to make a difference in my financial situation. Despite these obstacles, I continue to persevere and push forward, determined to make the most of my life and create opportunities for myself.

One of the most important aspects of my life is my desire to make a statement and have my voice heard. I am not content to simply accept the limitations that have been placed on me. I believe that my experiences and my resilience in the face of adversity can serve as an inspiration to others, showing that it is possible to overcome challenges and live a fulfilling life, even when the odds are stacked against you.

In this chapter, I hope to convey the importance of maintaining one's determination and spirit, even when faced with seemingly insurmountable obstacles. No matter what life throws at you, it is essential to keep pushing forward, embracing the challenges and seeking out new opportunities for growth and success.

Music – A Lifelong Love and Lessons Learned

Here, I explore my deep-rooted love for music and the lessons I've learned from my experiences in the music industry. My passion for music was ignited early in my life, as my father was a gospel singer. Growing up, I was surrounded by music and spent much of my time in church, where I was exposed to a wide range of musical styles and influences.

However, as I pursued my interests in the music industry, I quickly discovered that the business side of things could be quite challenging. I encountered numerous obstacles and setbacks, many of which stemmed from the individuals with whom I worked. One of the most significant issues I faced was the struggle for control and the desire for things to be done a certain way.

Despite these challenges, my love for music remained strong. I continued to immerse myself in the art form, exploring different genres, honing my skills, and seeking out new opportunities for creative expression. Through these experiences, I learned valuable lessons about perseverance, collaboration, and the importance of staying true to one's artistic vision.

Sharing my insights and experiences from my journey in the music industry, my goal here is to provide a glimpse into the challenges and rewards that come with pursuing a creative passion. While the path may not always be easy, the lessons learned and the personal growth achieved along the way make it a worthwhile endeavor.

The Atlanta Adventure and Meeting Tony Robbins

Here, I want to recount an unforgettable experience that took me to Atlanta, where I had the opportunity to meet the renowned motivational speaker, Tony Robbins. A friend had invited me to one of Robbins' seminars, and while sitting in the audience, I was unexpectedly called up on stage by Robbins himself.

Tony shared a bit about me and my passion for music with the audience, then made a surprising announcement: he pledged to give me ten thousand dollars towards my music and promised to introduce me to the legendary Quincy Jones. This was an incredible moment for me, and I was eager to make the most of the opportunity.

With the funds from Tony Robbins, I brought my team up from DC, rented cars and hotels, and ensured everyone was comfortable. We spent our time in Atlanta recording music and filming music videos. However, things took an unexpected turn when one of the team members, who had control over the music, pulled out at the last minute. His reason? He didn't trust another member of our group. This happened right after I had spent all that moncy on recording and mastering our music.

Although the situation didn't pan out as I had hoped, I still appreciate the opportunity and support Tony Robbins provided. Despite the challenges and setbacks, this experience taught me valuable lessons about trust, collaboration, and the unpredictable nature of the music industry. It also serves as a reminder that sometimes, even when things don't go according to plan, you can still learn and grow from the experience.

A Passion for Motivating Others

In this chapter, I discuss my love for motivating and inspiring people through public speaking. Standing in front of an audience and sharing my story gives me immense satisfaction, as it often provides a new perspective for those who may be struggling with their own challenges. Seeing their reactions and knowing that my words can have a profound impact on others is a truly rewarding experience.

At first, I didn't expect any compensation for my motivational speeches, as my passion for making a difference in people's lives outweighed any financial concerns. I genuinely looked forward to every opportunity to speak with organizations or visit classrooms, embracing the chance to share my story and motivate others.

However, as time went on, I realized that I needed to balance my passion with the practical reality of supporting myself. I decided to put a price on my speaking engagements, not out of greed, but as a recognition of the time, energy, and value I brought to those who listened to me. This decision was not an easy one, but it allowed me to continue pursuing my passion while also meeting my financial needs.

Through this journey, I learned the importance of valuing my time and expertise, even in the pursuit of my passions.

This chapter serves as a reminder that it's possible to balance personal fulfillment with practical considerations, as long as we remain focused on our ultimate goal: making a difference in the lives of others.

The Changing Nature of Friendships

This chapter explores the intricate nature of relationships, with a specific focus on the evolution of friendships and how they transform over time. I have experienced firsthand the pain and disappointment of backstabbing friends and have struggled to maintain trust in those around me.

I share a story of a male friend who not only spread lies about me to one of my girlfriends but also constantly intruded into my personal time with another. These experiences made me wary of people's intentions and motives, as it seemed that friendships were no longer as genuine as they once were.

However, I also acknowledge that life circumstances can play a significant role in the changing dynamics of friendships. As we grow older, our priorities shift, and we often find ourselves juggling responsibilities like marriage, children, and work. These commitments can leave us with less time and energy to devote to our friends and family, which can strain even the strongest of bonds.

Despite these challenges, I have learned that it is crucial to give people a chance to be trusted and to maintain an open heart. This chapter serves as a reminder that relationships are complex and ever-evolving, but they remain a vital aspect of our lives.

By staying vigilant and nurturing the connections we have, we can continue to find support and companionship in the people who truly matter.

Me & My Friend Chris Webber

Turning Adversity into Opportunity

I want to discuss the importance of self-awareness and the power of overcoming adversity. I share my personal experiences of facing challenges and finding ways to make things happen despite the odds stacked against me.

Throughout my life, I have been acutely aware of my financial limitations and the physical challenges I face daily. Yet, instead of allowing these obstacles to deter me, I have used them as a driving force to achieve my goals and secure the things I need to survive.

I emphasize the importance of having a clear understanding of one's purpose and the determination to pursue it relentlessly. By refusing to let setbacks derail me, I have managed to stay on track and focus on the bigger picture.

The key to my resilience is the mindset that life is happening for me, not to me. This perspective has allowed me to view my experiences as opportunities for growth rather than barriers to success. In this chapter, I offer a powerful reminder that we all have the power to shape our destinies and turn adversity into opportunity, no matter the challenges we face.

Always Ready 4 An Opportunity

Key Life Lessons, Shared Success, and Experiences

H ere, I want to examine the key lessons I've learned in life, along with the shared successes and experiences that have shaped me. One critical lesson I've learned is to never wait until the last minute to handle important matters. Procrastination is a significant pet peeve of mine. Since every day is an obstacle for me, there's no calm period to address these challenges. They must be tackled promptly and decisively.

Another crucial aspect of my journey has been maintaining my mental state. Keeping my mental health in check is essential, as the world can be relentless and unforgiving. The metaphorical "devil" never sleeps and continuously tries to pull us in different directions. That's why I prioritize strengthening my mental resilience and protecting my energy on all levels. This chapter will explore these life lessons and the shared experiences that have contributed to my growth and personal development.

Goals, Aspirations, and Self-Discovery

Heading toward the finish line, I will discuss my goals and aspirations, focusing on achieving financial stability to help others and spread my message of "No Excuses." My mission is to inspire people through my Motion and Motivations philosophy, which emphasizes the importance of staying in motion to motivate others. Rather than dwelling on my challenges, I choose to move forward and find motivation in the process.

My aspirations also include helping people maintain a level-headed approach to life. The world is often uneven, just like the grassy land around us, and it's vital to help others navigate its bumps and curves. I strive to be a supportive figure to those around me, sharing my experiences and offering guidance.

One example involves a young person in my community who was struggling with his relationship with his father. By sharing my own experiences of loss and encouraging him to see the bigger picture, I helped him gain a fresh perspective on the situation. My cousin Sean, who also lost his father, offered similar advice, emphasizing the importance of cherishing the time we have with our loved ones.

In this chapter I wanted to explore the journey of self-discovery and growth that has accompanied my pursuit of these goals and aspirations, as well as the impact they have had on the people around me.

Me & My Pops

Managing Anger and Embracing Gratitude

At one point in my life, I had to investigate and look into my journey of managing anger and learning to approach situations with a more positive outlook. I will discuss how I used to lash out and let my emotions take control, often viewing challenges from a negative perspective.

Over time, I realized that constantly focusing on the worst possible outcomes only hindered my ability to find solutions. To overcome this, I worked on changing my attitude and replacing negative thoughts with gratitude. By appreciating the good things in life and learning to approach challenges with a level head, I have found that my overall well-being has improved.

Researching the strategies and techniques I used to gain better control over my emotions and the impact that embracing gratitude has had on my personal and professional relationships. Additionally, here I wanted to discuss the importance of maintaining a positive mindset in overcoming life's challenges and staying resilient in the face of adversity.

No Excuses - A Message of Perseverance and Resilience

In this concluding chapter, I aim to leave you, my readers, with a powerful message to carry forward in your own lives: there are no excuses. By sharing my personal experiences and journey, I hope to inspire you to never give up on your dreams and to always persevere, regardless of the obstacles you face.

We will reflect on the key lessons learned throughout the book, emphasizing the importance of staying on course and remaining focused on what truly matters. I encourage you to confront your own challenges head-on, and to use my story as a source of motivation in your quest for personal and professional fulfillment.

Ultimately, the question I pose to you, my dear readers, is this: What's your excuse?

It is my hope that by reading my story, you will find the strength to overcome any barriers in your path, and to embrace life with unwavering determination and resilience.

A Life Told in Pictures

Me at 5

Chillin' in Sunday's Best

Working & Networking

Chillin' By the Water

Chapter 43

If You Only Knew the Half

Byron "Soulja" Breeze